Test 1b

D0997543

1. $12 \div 4 = *$

2. $10 \div 2 = *$

3. $15 \div 3 = *$

4. $16 \div 4 = *$

5. $6 \div 2 = *$

6. $27 \div 3 = *$

7. $8 \div 4 = *$

8. $16 \div 2 = *$

9. $30 \div 3 = *$

10. $20 \div 4 = *$

11. $4 \div 2 = *$

12. $12 \div 3 = *$

13. $24 \div 4 = *$

14. $21 \div 3 = *$

15. $20 \div 2 = *$

16. $12 \div 2 = *$

17. $6 \div 3 = *$

18. $36 \div 4 = *$

19. $9 \div 3 = *$

20. $14 \div 2 = *$

Do not write in this space.

Place a sheet of scrap paper here and write your answers on that.

Always remember to time yourself for each test.

Write your score out of 20 and your time in minutes and seconds on the Record Sheet at the back of this book.

Test 1c

1. * x 3 = 21

2. 12 ÷ * = 2

3. 4 x * = 20

4. * ÷ 2 = 5

5. * x 3 = 9

6. 12 ÷ * = 4

7. 7 x * = 14

8. * ÷ 3 = 9

9. * x 4 = 8

10. 6 ÷ * = 2

11. 3 x * = 15

12. * ÷ 4 = 4

13. * x 2 = 20

14. 30 ÷ * = 10

15. 4 x * = 36

16. * ÷ 2 = 8

17. * x 3 = 12

18. 24 ÷ * = 4

19. 2 x * = 4

20. * ÷ 3 = 7

Do not write in this space.

Place a sheet of scrap paper here and write your answers on that.

Always remember to time yourself for each test.

Write your score out of 20 and your time in minutes and seconds on the Record Sheet at the back of this book.

Test 2a

1. $10 \times 4 = *$

2. $4 \times 2 = *$

3. $8 \times 3 = *$

4. $7 \times 4 = *$

5. $5 \times 2 = *$

6. $6 \times 3 = *$

7. $4 \times 4 = *$

8. $9 \times 2 = *$

9. $3 \times 3 = *$

10. $8 \times 4 = *$

11. $6 \times 2 = *$

12. $5 \times 3 = *$

13. $3 \times 4 = *$

14. $8 \times 2 = *$

15. $9 \times 3 = *$

16. $6 \times 4 = *$

17. $2 \times 2 = *$

18. $10 \times 3 = *$

19. $9 \times 4 = *$

20. $7 \times 2 = *$

Do not write in this space.

Place a sheet of scrap paper here and write your answers on that.

Always remember to time yourself for each test.

Write your score out of 20 and your time in minutes and seconds on the Record Sheet at the back of this book.

Test 2b

1 $4 \div 2 = *$

2 $9 \div 3 = *$

3 $12 \div 4 = *$

4 $18 \div 3 = *$

5 $16 \div 4 = *$

6 $8 \div 2 = *$

7 $16 \div 2 = *$

8 $27 \div 3 = *$

9 $40 \div 4 = *$

10 $15 \div 3 = *$

11 $12 \div 2 = *$

12 $24 \div 4 = *$

13 $30 \div 3 = *$

14 $14 \div 2 = *$

15 $32 \div 4 = *$

16 $18 \div 2 = *$

17 $24 \div 3 = *$

18 $28 \div 4 = *$

19 $10 \div 2 = *$

20 $36 \div 4 = *$

Do not write in this space.

Place a sheet of scrap paper here and write your answers on that.

Always remember to time yourself for each test.

Write your score out of 20 and your time in minutes and seconds on the Record Sheet at the back of this book.

Test 2c

1 * x 3 = 15

2 4 ÷ * = 2

3 4 x * = 16

4 * ÷ 3 = 6

5 * x 2 = 12

6 14 ÷ * = 7

7 3 x * = 9

8 * ÷ 3 = 8

9 * x 2 = 8

10 40 ÷ * = 10

11 8 x * = 16

12 * ÷ 3 = 4

13 * x 3 = 27

14 24 ÷ * = 6

15 2 x * = 10

16 * ÷ 2 = 9

17 * x 4 = 32

18 30 ÷ * = 10

19 4 x * = 36

20 * ÷ 4 = 7

Do not write in this space.

Place a sheet of scrap paper here and write your answers on that.

Always remember to time yourself for each test.

Write your score out of 20 and your time in minutes and seconds on the Record Sheet at the back of this book.

Test 3a

1 $6 \times 3 = *$

2 $8 \times 4 = *$

3 $2 \times 5 = *$

4 $2 \times 3 = *$

5 $5 \times 4 = *$

6 $7 \times 5 = *$

7 $8 \times 2 = *$

8 $7 \times 3 = *$

9 $10 \times 0 = *$

10 $3 \times 5 = *$

11 $4 \times 3 = *$

12 $7 \times 4 = *$

13 $5 \times 5 = *$

14 $9 \times 2 = *$

15 $8 \times 3 = *$

16 $2 \times 4 = *$

17 $8 \times 5 = *$

18 $9 \times 3 = *$

19 $4 \times 4 = *$

20 $6 \times 5 = *$

Do not write in this space.

Place a sheet of scrap paper here and write your answers on that.

Always remember to time yourself for each test.

Write your score out of 20 and your time in minutes and seconds on the Record Sheet at the back of this book.

Test 3b

1. $6 \div 3 = *$

2. $16 \div 4 = *$

3. $18 \div 2 = *$

4. $15 \div 5 = *$

5. $21 \div 3 = *$

6. $8 \div 4 = *$

7. $27 \div 3 = *$

8. $10 \div 5 = *$

9. $18 \div 3 = *$

10. $30 \div 5 = *$

11. $28 \div 4 = *$

12. $12 \div 3 = *$

13. $16 \div 2 = *$

14. $20 \div 4 = *$

15. $25 \div 5 = *$

16. $20 \div 1 = *$

17. $35 \div 5 = *$

18. $32 \div 4 = *$

19. $24 \div 3 = *$

20. $40 \div 5 = *$

Do not write in this space.

Place a sheet of scrap paper here and write your answers on that.

Always remember to time yourself for each test.

Write your score out of 20 and your time in minutes and seconds on the Record Sheet at the back of this book.

Test 3c

1. * x 3 = 6

2. 8 ÷ * = 4

3. 4 x * = 16

4. * ÷ 3 = 7

5. * x 5 = 10

6. 12 ÷ * = 3

7. 6 x * = 18

8. * ÷ 5 = 5

9. * x 3 = 27

10. 15 ÷ * = 5

11. 7 x * = 28

12. * ÷ 2 = 8

13. * x 5 = 35

14. 32 ÷ * = 8

15. 10 x * = 40

16. * ÷ 2 = 9

17. * x 5 = 30

18. 20 ÷ * = 4

19. 8 x * = 24

20. * ÷ 5 = 8

Do not write in this space.

Place a sheet of scrap paper here and write your answers on that.

Always remember to time yourself for each test.

Write your score out of 20 and your time in minutes and seconds on the Record Sheet at the back of this book.

Test 4a

1. $3 \times 3 = *$

2. $8 \times 4 = *$

3. $4 \times 5 = *$

4. $7 \times 3 = *$

5. $5 \times 4 = *$

6. $9 \times 5 = *$

7. $5 \times 3 = *$

8. $9 \times 4 = *$

9. $10 \times 5 = *$

10. $7 \times 2 = *$

11. $4 \times 3 = *$

12. $6 \times 0 = *$

13. $3 \times 5 = *$

14. $6 \times 3 = *$

15. $7 \times 4 = *$

16. $8 \times 5 = *$

17. $8 \times 3 = *$

18. $3 \times 4 = *$

19. $5 \times 5 = *$

20. $10 \times 4 = *$

Do not write in this space.

Place a sheet of scrap paper here and write your answers on that.

Always remember to time yourself for each test.

Write your score out of 20 and your time in minutes and seconds on the Record Sheet at the back of this book.

Test 4b

1. $15 \div 3 = *$
2. $14 \div 2 = *$
3. $12 \div 4 = *$
4. $25 \div 5 = *$
5. $12 \div 3 = *$
6. $20 \div 4 = *$
7. $18 \div 3 = *$
8. $28 \div 4 = *$
9. $20 \div 5 = *$
10. $9 \div 3 = *$
11. $50 \div 5 = *$
12. $24 \div 4 = *$
13. $24 \div 3 = *$
14. $40 \div 4 = *$
15. $15 \div 5 = *$
16. $21 \div 3 = *$
17. $40 \div 5 = *$
18. $36 \div 4 = *$
19. $45 \div 5 = *$
20. $32 \div 4 = *$

Do not write in this space.

Place a sheet of scrap paper here and write your answers on that.

Always remember to time yourself for each test.

Write your score out of 20 and your time in minutes and seconds on the Record Sheet at the back of this book.

Test 4c

1. $* \times 5 = 20$

2. $12 \div * = 3$

3. $4 \times * = 40$

4. $* \div 5 = 3$

5. $* \times 3 = 9$

6. $14 \div * = 2$

7. $3 \times * = 24$

8. $* \div 5 = 5$

9. $* \times 4 = 20$

10. $21 \div * = 3$

11. $5 \times * = 40$

12. $* \div 4 = 7$

13. $* \times 4 = 12$

14. $18 \div * = 3$

15. $4 \times * = 36$

16. $* \div 3 = 5$

17. $* \times 4 = 24$

18. $45 \div * = 5$

19. $5 \times * = 50$

20. $* \div 4 = 8$

Do not write in this space.

Place a sheet of scrap paper here and write your answers on that.

Always remember to time yourself for each test.

Write your score out of 20 and your time in minutes and seconds on the Record Sheet at the back of this book.

Test 5a

1. $2 \times 4 = *$

2. $9 \times 5 = *$

3. $5 \times 2 = *$

4. $6 \times 5 = *$

5. $3 \times 6 = *$

6. $7 \times 4 = *$

7. $4 \times 5 = *$

8. $6 \times 6 = *$

9. $5 \times 4 = *$

10. $7 \times 5 = *$

11. $2 \times 6 = *$

12. $4 \times 4 = *$

13. $2 \times 5 = *$

14. $8 \times 6 = *$

15. $9 \times 4 = *$

16. $8 \times 5 = *$

17. $3 \times 5 = *$

18. $4 \times 6 = *$

19. $8 \times 4 = *$

20. $5 \times 5 = *$

Do not write in this space.

Place a sheet of scrap paper here and write your answers on that.

Always remember to time yourself for each test.

Write your score out of 20 and your time in minutes and seconds on the Record Sheet at the back of this book.

Test 5b

1. $10 \div 5 = *$

2. $12 \div 6 = *$

3. $24 \div 6 = *$

4. $20 \div 5 = *$

5. $18 \div 6 = *$

6. $10 \div 2 = *$

7. $20 \div 4 = *$

8. $30 \div 5 = *$

9. $8 \div 4 = *$

10. $16 \div 4 = *$

11. $25 \div 5 = *$

12. $15 \div 5 = *$

13. $36 \div 6 = *$

14. $28 \div 4 = *$

15. $40 \div 5 = *$

16. $48 \div 6 = *$

17. $35 \div 5 = *$

18. $36 \div 4 = *$

19. $32 \div 4 = *$

20. $45 \div 5 = *$

Do not write in this space.

Place a sheet of scrap paper here and write your answers on that.

Always remember to time yourself for each test.

Write your score out of 20 and your time in minutes and seconds on the Record Sheet at the back of this book.

Test 5c

1. * x 2 = 10

2. 20 ÷ * = 4

3. 5 x * = 15

4. * ÷ 2 = 6

5. * x 5 = 30

6. 8 ÷ * = 4

7. 5 x * = 30

8. * ÷ 2 = 5

9. * x 4 = 16

10. 20 ÷ * = 5

11. 5 x * = 40

12. * ÷ 6 = 6

13. * x 4 = 32

14. 35 ÷ * = 5

15. 6 x * = 18

16. * ÷ 4 = 7

17. * x 6 = 48

18. 36 ÷ * = 4

19. 6 x * = 24

20. * ÷ 5 = 9

Do not write in this space.

Place a sheet of scrap paper here and write your answers on that.

Always remember to time yourself for each test.

Write your score out of 20 and your time in minutes and seconds on the Record Sheet at the back of this book.

Test 6a

1   $5 \times 6 = *$

2   $6 \times 2 = *$

3   $9 \times 3 = *$

4   $6 \times 4 = *$

5   $4 \times 5 = *$

6   $7 \times 6 = *$

7   $2 \times 3 = *$

8   $8 \times 5 = *$

9   $9 \times 6 = *$

10 $2 \times 5 = *$

11 $3 \times 6 = *$

12 $3 \times 4 = *$

13 $5 \times 5 = *$

14 $10 \times 6 = *$

15 $7 \times 5 = *$

16 $2 \times 6 = *$

17 $8 \times 3 = *$

18 $7 \times 4 = *$

19 $9 \times 5 = *$

20 $6 \times 6 = *$

Do not write in this space.

Place a sheet of scrap paper here and write your answers on that.

Always remember to time yourself for each test.

Write your score out of 20 and your time in minutes and seconds on the Record Sheet at the back of this book.

Test 6b

1 $12 \div 6 = *$

2 $20 \div 5 = *$

3 $24 \div 3 = *$

4 $6 \div 3 = *$

5 $30 \div 6 = *$

6 $25 \div 5 = *$

7 $28 \div 4 = *$

8 $36 \div 6 = *$

9 $10 \div 5 = *$

10 $24 \div 4 = *$

11 $12 \div 2 = *$

12 $35 \div 5 = *$

13 $60 \div 6 = *$

14 $45 \div 5 = *$

15 $42 \div 6 = *$

16 $27 \div 3 = *$

17 $18 \div 6 = *$

18 $54 \div 6 = *$

19 $40 \div 5 = *$

20 $12 \div 4 = *$

Do not write in this space.

Place a sheet of scrap paper here and write your answers on that.

Always remember to time yourself for each test.

Write your score out of 20 and your time in minutes and seconds on the Record Sheet at the back of this book.

Test 6c

1. $* \times 3 = 6$

2. $12 \div * = 4$

3. $5 \times * = 45$

4. $* \div 4 = 5$

5. $* \times 2 = 12$

6. $25 \div * = 5$

7. $3 \times * = 24$

8. $* \div 6 = 9$

9. $* \times 4 = 24$

10. $36 \div * = 6$

11. $3 \times * = 9$

12. $* \div 6 = 5$

13. $* \times 5 = 40$

14. $18 \div * = 6$

15. $5 \times * = 35$

16. $* \div 6 = 7$

17. $* \times 4 = 28$

18. $60 \div * = 6$

19. $5 \times * = 10$

20. $* \div 2 = 6$

Do not write in this space.

Place a sheet of scrap paper here and write your answers on that.

Always remember to time yourself for each test.

Write your score out of 20 and your time in minutes and seconds on the Record Sheet at the back of this book.

Test 7a

1. $1 \times 5 = *$
2. $4 \times 6 = *$
3. $9 \times 2 = *$
4. $3 \times 3 = *$
5. $8 \times 4 = *$
6. $5 \times 5 = *$
7. $7 \times 0 = *$
8. $6 \times 5 = *$
9. $8 \times 6 = *$
10. $2 \times 7 = *$
11. $3 \times 5 = *$
12. $9 \times 6 = *$
13. $5 \times 7 = *$
14. $8 \times 5 = *$
15. $5 \times 6 = *$
16. $3 \times 7 = *$
17. $4 \times 5 = *$
18. $3 \times 6 = *$
19. $7 \times 7 = *$
20. $10 \times 6 = *$

Do not write in this space.

Place a sheet of scrap paper here and write your answers on that.

Always remember to time yourself for each test.

Write your score out of 20 and your time in minutes and seconds on the Record Sheet at the back of this book.

Test 7b

1. $14 \div 7 = *$

2. $25 \div 5 = *$

3. $30 \div 6 = *$

4. $54 \div 6 = *$

5. $9 \div 3 = *$

6. $24 \div 6 = *$

7. $40 \div 5 = *$

8. $18 \div 6 = *$

9. $49 \div 7 = *$

10. $48 \div 6 = *$

11. $18 \div 2 = *$

12. $21 \div 7 = *$

13. $60 \div 6 = *$

14. $20 \div 5 = *$

15. $35 \div 7 = *$

16. $15 \div 5 = *$

17. $42 \div 6 = *$

18. $32 \div 4 = *$

19. $5 \div 1 = *$

20. $30 \div 5 = *$

Do not write in this space.

Place a sheet of scrap paper here and write your answers on that.

Always remember to time yourself for each test.

Write your score out of 20 and your time in minutes and seconds on the Record Sheet at the back of this book.

Test 7c

1.   *   x   3   =   9

2.   15   ÷   *   =   5

3.   6   x   *   =   18

4.   *   ÷   5   =   7

5.   *   x   6   =   24

6.   40   ÷   *   =   5

7.   7   x   *   =   0

8.   *   ÷   9   =   2

9.   *   x   1   =   5

10.   32   ÷   *   =   4

11.   6   x   *   =   54

12.   *   ÷   4   =   5

13.   *   x   6   =   60

14.   49   ÷   *   =   7

15.   5   x   *   =   25

16.   *   ÷   2   =   7

17.   *   x   5   =   30

18.   48   ÷   *   =   6

19.   6   x   *   =   30

20.   *   ÷   3   =   7

Do not write in this space.

Place a sheet of scrap paper here and write your answers on that.

Always remember to time yourself for each test.

Write your score out of 20 and your time in minutes and seconds on the Record Sheet at the back of this book.

Test 8a

1. 2 x 6 = *

2. 4 x 7 = *

3. 7 x 5 = *

4. 6 x 6 = *

5. 9 x 7 = *

6. 9 x 5 = *

7. 10 x 6 = *

8. 6 x 7 = *

9. 2 x 5 = *

10. 4 x 6 = *

11. 10 x 7 = *

12. 4 x 2 = *

13. 5 x 3 = *

14. 9 x 4 = *

15. 5 x 5 = *

16. 7 x 6 = *

17. 8 x 7 = *

18. 10 x 5 = *

19. 5 x 6 = *

20. 5 x 7 = *

Do not write in this space.

Place a sheet of scrap paper here and write your answers on that.

Always remember to time yourself for each test.

Write your score out of 20 and your time in minutes and seconds on the Record Sheet at the back of this book.

Test 8b

1. $10 \div 5 = *$

2. $28 \div 7 = *$

3. $36 \div 4 = *$

4. $56 \div 7 = *$

5. $8 \div 2 = *$

6. $60 \div 6 = *$

7. $63 \div 7 = *$

8. $12 \div 6 = *$

9. $25 \div 5 = *$

10. $50 \div 5 = *$

11. $35 \div 7 = *$

12. $36 \div 6 = *$

13. $24 \div 6 = *$

14. $15 \div 3 = *$

15. $42 \div 6 = *$

16. $70 \div 7 = *$

17. $30 \div 6 = *$

18. $45 \div 5 = *$

19. $42 \div 7 = *$

20. $35 \div 5 = *$

Do not write in this space.

Place a sheet of scrap paper here and write your answers on that.

Always remember to time yourself for each test.

Write your score out of 20 and your time in minutes and seconds on the Record Sheet at the back of this book.

Test 8c

1 * x 5 = 50

2 8 ÷ * = 2

3 7 x * = 63

4 * ÷ 2 = 6

5 * x 3 = 15

6 56 ÷ * = 7

7 5 x * = 10

8 * ÷ 6 = 6

9 * x 7 = 28

10 36 ÷ * = 4

11 5 x * = 25

12 * ÷ 5 = 6

13 * x 5 = 45

14 42 ÷ * = 6

15 7 x * = 35

16 * ÷ 4 = 6

17 * x 5 = 35

18 60 ÷ * = 6

19 7 x * = 70

20 * ÷ 6 = 7

Do not write in this space.

Place a sheet of scrap paper here and write your answers on that.

Always remember to time yourself for each test.

Write your score out of 20 and your time in minutes and seconds on the Record Sheet at the back of this book.

Test 9a

1   6 x 5 = *

2   8 x 6 = *

3   3 x 7 = *

4   8 x 5 = *

5   9 x 6 = *

6   7 x 7 = *

7   6 x 6 = *

8   4 x 7 = *

9   3 x 8 = *

10   2 x 5 = *

11   7 x 6 = *

12   2 x 7 = *

13   9 x 5 = *

14   6 x 8 = *

15   6 x 7 = *

16   5 x 8 = *

17   3 x 6 = *

18   8 x 7 = *

19   2 x 8 = *

20   9 x 7 = *

Do not write in
this space.

Place a sheet of
scrap paper here
and write your
answers on that.

Always remember
to time yourself
for each test.

Write your score
out of 20 and
your time in
minutes and
seconds on the
Record Sheet
at the back of
this book.

Test 9b

1. $56 \div 7 = *$

2. $36 \div 6 = *$

3. $40 \div 5 = *$

4. $14 \div 7 = *$

5. $40 \div 8 = *$

6. $16 \div 8 = *$

7. $28 \div 7 = *$

8. $48 \div 6 = *$

9. $30 \div 5 = *$

10. $21 \div 7 = *$

11. $18 \div 6 = *$

12. $63 \div 7 = *$

13. $45 \div 5 = *$

14. $48 \div 8 = *$

15. $10 \div 5 = *$

16. $24 \div 8 = *$

17. $49 \div 7 = *$

18. $42 \div 6 = *$

19. $54 \div 6 = *$

20. $42 \div 7 = *$

Do not write in this space.

Place a sheet of scrap paper here and write your answers on that.

Always remember to time yourself for each test.

Write your score out of 20 and your time in minutes and seconds on the Record Sheet at the back of this book.

Test 9c

1. $* \times 7 = 21$

2. $24 \div * = 8$

3. $6 \times * = 18$

4. $* \div 6 = 5$

5. $* \times 6 = 42$

6. $16 \div * = 8$

7. $5 \times * = 45$

8. $* \div 7 = 7$

9. $* \times 6 = 48$

10. $63 \div * = 7$

11. $8 \times * = 40$

12. $* \div 6 = 6$

13. $* \times 5 = 40$

14. $14 \div * = 7$

15. $8 \times * = 48$

16. $* \div 8 = 7$

17. $* \times 5 = 10$

18. $28 \div * = 7$

19. $6 \times * = 54$

20. $* \div 7 = 6$

Do not write in this space.

Place a sheet of scrap paper here and write your answers on that.

Always remember to time yourself for each test.

Write your score out of 20 and your time in minutes and seconds on the Record Sheet at the back of this book.

Test 10a

1   4 x 8 = *

2   9 x 6 = *

3   10 x 7 = *

4   6 x 8 = *

5   5 x 6 = *

6   2 x 7 = *

7   8 x 8 = *

8   6 x 0 = *

9   5 x 7 = *

10   7 x 8 = *

11   4 x 6 = *

12   9 x 7 = *

13   10 x 8 = *

14   7 x 6 = *

15   3 x 7 = *

16   9 x 8 = *

17   2 x 6 = *

18   6 x 7 = *

19   5 x 8 = *

20   10 x 6 = *

Do not write in this space.

Place a sheet of scrap paper here and write your answers on that.

Always remember to time yourself for each test.

Write your score out of 20 and your time in minutes and seconds on the Record Sheet at the back of this book.

Test 10b

1. $80 \div 8 = *$

2. $14 \div 7 = *$

3. $54 \div 6 = *$

4. $35 \div 7 = *$

5. $72 \div 8 = *$

6. $12 \div 6 = *$

7. $40 \div 8 = *$

8. $21 \div 7 = *$

9. $36 \div 6 = *$

10. $48 \div 8 = *$

11. $70 \div 7 = *$

12. $32 \div 8 = *$

13. $42 \div 6 = *$

14. $56 \div 8 = *$

15. $30 \div 6 = *$

16. $63 \div 7 = *$

17. $24 \div 6 = *$

18. $42 \div 7 = *$

19. $60 \div 6 = *$

20. $64 \div 8 = *$

Do not write in this space.

Place a sheet of scrap paper here and write your answers on that.

Always remember to time yourself for each test.

Write your score out of 20 and your time in minutes and seconds on the Record Sheet at the back of this book.

Test 10c

1. $* \times 8 = 40$

2. $24 \div * = 6$

3. $7 \times * = 14$

4. $* \div 6 = 9$

5. $* \times 7 = 35$

6. $12 \div * = 6$

7. $7 \times * = 21$

8. $* \div 8 = 10$

9. $* \times 6 = 0$

10. $32 \div * = 8$

11. $7 \times * = 70$

12. $* \div 6 = 7$

13. $* \times 8 = 72$

14. $30 \div * = 6$

15. $8 \times * = 64$

16. $* \div 7 = 9$

17. $* \times 6 = 60$

18. $56 \div * = 8$

19. $6 \times * = 42$

20. $* \div 6 = 8$

Do not write in this space.

Place a sheet of scrap paper here and write your answers on that.

Always remember to time yourself for each test.

Write your score out of 20 and your time in minutes and seconds on the Record Sheet at the back of this book.

Test 11a

1   7 x 7 = *

2   8 x 8 = *

3   6 x 6 = *

4   5 x 5 = *

5   4 x 7 = *

6   3 x 8 = *

7   2 x 9 = *

8   8 x 7 = *

9   4 x 8 = *

10   5 x 9 = *

11   10 x 1 = *

12   2 x 8 = *

13   9 x 9 = *

14   5 x 7 = *

15   6 x 8 = *

16   3 x 9 = *

17   6 x 7 = *

18   9 x 8 = *

19   4 x 9 = *

20   10 x 8 = *

Do not write in this space.

Place a sheet of scrap paper here and write your answers on that.

Always remember to time yourself for each test.

Write your score out of 20 and your time in minutes and seconds on the Record Sheet at the back of this book.

Test 11b

1. $45 \div 9 = *$

2. $48 \div 8 = *$

3. $25 \div 5 = *$

4. $32 \div 8 = *$

5. $36 \div 9 = *$

6. $70 \div 7 = *$

7. $64 \div 8 = *$

8. $27 \div 9 = *$

9. $56 \div 7 = *$

10. $80 \div 8 = *$

11. $18 \div 9 = *$

12. $36 \div 6 = *$

13. $35 \div 7 = *$

14. $72 \div 8 = *$

15. $81 \div 9 = *$

16. $24 \div 8 = *$

17. $42 \div 7 = *$

18. $16 \div 8 = *$

19. $28 \div 7 = *$

20. $49 \div 7 = *$

Do not write in this space.

Place a sheet of scrap paper here and write your answers on that.

Always remember to time yourself for each test.

Write your score out of 20 and your time in minutes and seconds on the Record Sheet at the back of this book.

Test 11c

1. * x 9 = 81

2. 48 ÷ * = 8

3. 6 x * = 36

4. * ÷ 4 = 9

5. * x 10 = 100

6. 18 ÷ * = 9

7. 7 x * = 49

8. * ÷ 8 = 6

9. * x 8 = 80

10. 35 ÷ * = 7

11. 8 x * = 24

12. * ÷ 5 = 5

13. * x 9 = 27

14. 42 ÷ * = 7

15. 8 x * = 64

16. * ÷ 9 = 5

17. * x 8 = 16

18. 56 ÷ * = 7

19. 8 x * = 72

20. * ÷ 7 = 4

Do not write in this space.

Place a sheet of scrap paper here and write your answers on that.

Always remember to time yourself for each test.

Write your score out of 20 and your time in minutes and seconds on the Record Sheet at the back of this book.

Test 12a

1 6 x 9 = *

2 3 x 7 = *

3 7 x 8 = *

4 10 x 9 = *

5 6 x 7 = *

6 2 x 8 = *

7 7 x 9 = *

8 7 x 7 = *

9 8 x 8 = *

10 8 x 9 = *

11 3 x 8 = *

12 5 x 9 = *

13 6 x 8 = *

14 9 x 7 = *

15 4 x 8 = *

16 9 x 9 = *

17 2 x 7 = *

18 8 x 7 = *

19 2 x 9 = *

20 9 x 8 = *

Do not write in this space.

Place a sheet of scrap paper here and write your answers on that.

Always remember to time yourself for each test.

Write your score out of 20 and your time in minutes and seconds on the Record Sheet at the back of this book.

Test 12b

1. $24 \div 8 = *$

2. $81 \div 9 = *$

3. $21 \div 7 = *$

4. $63 \div 9 = *$

5. $32 \div 8 = *$

6. $18 \div 9 = *$

7. $42 \div 7 = *$

8. $56 \div 8 = *$

9. $45 \div 9 = *$

10. $63 \div 7 = *$

11. $14 \div 7 = *$

12. $72 \div 8 = *$

13. $54 \div 9 = *$

14. $64 \div 8 = *$

15. $72 \div 9 = *$

16. $48 \div 8 = *$

17. $90 \div 9 = *$

18. $16 \div 8 = *$

19. $56 \div 7 = *$

20. $49 \div 7 = *$

Do not write in this space.

Place a sheet of scrap paper here and write your answers on that.

Always remember to time yourself for each test.

Write your score out of 20 and your time in minutes and seconds on the Record Sheet at the back of this book.

Test 12c

1 * x 8 = 72

2 54 ÷ * = 9

3 8 x * = 16

4 * ÷ 9 = 8

5 * x 7 = 49

6 24 ÷ * = 8

7 9 x * = 18

8 * ÷ 7 = 2

9 * x 9 = 63

10 21 ÷ * = 7

11 8 x * = 48

12 * ÷ 9 = 9

13 * x 8 = 56

14 32 ÷ * = 8

15 9 x * = 45

16 * ÷ 6 = 7

17 * x 9 = 90

18 56 ÷ * = 8

19 7 x * = 63

20 * ÷ 8 = 8

Do not write in this space.

Place a sheet of scrap paper here and write your answers on that.

Always remember to time yourself for each test.

Write your score out of 20 and your time in minutes and seconds on the Record Sheet at the back of this book.

Test 13a

1. $3 \times 9 = *$

2. $4 \times 7 = *$

3. $5 \times 8 = *$

4. $7 \times 9 = *$

5. $9 \times 6 = *$

6. $13 \times 0 = *$

7. $7 \times 8 = *$

8. $6 \times 9 = *$

9. $8 \times 9 = *$

10. $8 \times 8 = *$

11. $4 \times 9 = *$

12. $8 \times 7 = *$

13. $9 \times 8 = *$

14. $2 \times 9 = *$

15. $9 \times 9 = *$

16. $2 \times 8 = *$

17. $5 \times 9 = *$

18. $3 \times 8 = *$

19. $6 \times 7 = *$

20. $6 \times 8 = *$

Do not write in this space.

Place a sheet of scrap paper here and write your answers on that.

Always remember to time yourself for each test.

Write your score out of 20 and your time in minutes and seconds on the Record Sheet at the back of this book.

Test 13b

1. $54 \div 9 = *$

2. $42 \div 7 = *$

3. $40 \div 8 = *$

4. $56 \div 7 = *$

5. $72 \div 9 = *$

6. $16 \div 8 = *$

7. $18 \div 9 = *$

8. $64 \div 8 = *$

9. $70 \div 7 = *$

10. $63 \div 9 = *$

11. $24 \div 8 = *$

12. $27 \div 9 = *$

13. $48 \div 8 = *$

14. $81 \div 9 = *$

15. $54 \div 6 = *$

16. $28 \div 7 = *$

17. $72 \div 8 = *$

18. $45 \div 9 = *$

19. $56 \div 8 = *$

20. $36 \div 9 = *$

Do not write in this space.

Place a sheet of scrap paper here and write your answers on that.

Always remember to time yourself for each test.

Write your score out of 20 and your time in minutes and seconds on the Record Sheet at the back of this book.

Test 13c

1. * x 9 = 45

2. 56 ÷ * = 7

3. 8 x * = 40

4. * ÷ 3 = 9

5. * x 8 = 64

6. 56 ÷ * = 8

7. 6 x * = 54

8. * ÷ 4 = 7

9. * x 8 = 48

10. 81 ÷ * = 9

11. 13 x * = 0

12. * ÷ 9 = 7

13. * x 8 = 72

14. 18 ÷ * = 9

15. 8 x * = 24

16. * ÷ 9 = 6

17. * x 8 = 16

18. 42 ÷ * = 7

19. 9 x * = 36

20. * ÷ 8 = 9

Do not write in this space.

Place a sheet of scrap paper here and write your answers on that.

Always remember to time yourself for each test.

Write your score out of 20 and your time in minutes and seconds on the Record Sheet at the back of this book.

Test 14a

1 4 x 9 = *

2 9 x 7 = *

3 6 x 8 = *

4 8 x 9 = *

5 2 x 7 = *

6 4 x 8 = *

7 9 x 6 = *

8 10 x 8 = *

9 9 x 9 = *

10 5 x 9 = *

11 10 x 9 = *

12 5 x 7 = *

13 8 x 8 = *

14 7 x 9 = *

15 9 x 8 = *

16 3 x 9 = *

17 6 x 9 = *

18 4 x 7 = *

19 2 x 9 = *

20 7 x 8 = *

Do not write in
this space.

Place a sheet of
scrap paper here
and write your
answers on that.

Always remember
to time yourself
for each test.

Write your score
out of 20 and
your time in
minutes and
seconds on the
Record Sheet
at the back of
this book.

Test 14b

1. $81 \div 9 = *$

2. $28 \div 7 = *$

3. $56 \div 8 = *$

4. $36 \div 9 = *$

5. $45 \div 9 = *$

6. $35 \div 7 = *$

7. $64 \div 8 = *$

8. $27 \div 9 = *$

9. $14 \div 7 = *$

10. $48 \div 8 = *$

11. $63 \div 7 = *$

12. $90 \div 9 = *$

13. $72 \div 8 = *$

14. $54 \div 9 = *$

15. $32 \div 8 = *$

16. $80 \div 8 = *$

17. $72 \div 9 = *$

18. $18 \div 9 = *$

19. $54 \div 6 = *$

20. $63 \div 9 = *$

Do not write in this space.

Place a sheet of scrap paper here and write your answers on that.

Always remember to time yourself for each test.

Write your score out of 20 and your time in minutes and seconds on the Record Sheet at the back of this book.

Test 14c

1. * x 6 = 54

2. 63 ÷ * = 7

3. 8 x * = 64

4. * ÷ 6 = 9

5. * x 7 = 35

6. 48 ÷ * = 8

7. 9 x * = 81

8. * ÷ 7 = 8

9. * x 7 = 28

10. 45 ÷ * = 9

11. 7 x * = 14

12. * ÷ 4 = 9

13. * x 8 = 72

14. 90 ÷ * = 9

15. 9 x * = 18

16. * ÷ 8 = 10

17. * x 9 = 63

18. 32 ÷ * = 8

19. 9 x * = 72

20. * ÷ 3 = 9

Do not write in this space.

Place a sheet of scrap paper here and write your answers on that.

Always remember to time yourself for each test.

Write your score out of 20 and your time in minutes and seconds on the Record Sheet at the back of this book.

Test 15a

1. $7 \times 9 = *$

2. $8 \times 6 = *$

3. $7 \times 8 = *$

4. $9 \times 4 = *$

5. $8 \times 8 = *$

6. $10 \times 10 = *$

7. $5 \times 8 = *$

8. $6 \times 9 = *$

9. $7 \times 4 = *$

10. $9 \times 3 = *$

11. $6 \times 5 = *$

12. $8 \times 9 = *$

13. $9 \times 6 = *$

14. $8 \times 3 = *$

15. $6 \times 7 = *$

16. $3 \times 9 = *$

17. $9 \times 5 = *$

18. $6 \times 8 = *$

19. $8 \times 7 = *$

20. $8 \times 4 = *$

Do not write in this space.

Place a sheet of scrap paper here and write your answers on that.

Always remember to time yourself for each test.

Write your score out of 20 and your time in minutes and seconds on the Record Sheet at the back of this book.

Test 15b

1 $10 \div 10 = *$

2 $30 \div 5 = *$

3 $42 \div 7 = *$

4 $32 \div 4 = *$

5 $64 \div 8 = *$

6 $48 \div 6 = *$

7 $45 \div 5 = *$

8 $56 \div 7 = *$

9 $40 \div 8 = *$

10 $27 \div 9 = *$

11 $54 \div 6 = *$

12 $24 \div 3 = *$

13 $48 \div 8 = *$

14 $28 \div 4 = *$

15 $63 \div 9 = *$

16 $27 \div 3 = *$

17 $54 \div 9 = *$

18 $36 \div 4 = *$

19 $56 \div 8 = *$

20 $72 \div 9 = *$

Do not write in this space.

Place a sheet of scrap paper here and write your answers on that.

Always remember to time yourself for each test.

Write your score out of 20 and your time in minutes and seconds on the Record Sheet at the back of this book.

Test 15c

1. * x 3 = 27

2. 64 ÷ * = 8

3. 5 x * = 45

4. * ÷ 9 = 6

5. * x 4 = 28

6. 10 ÷ * = 10

7. 4 x * = 32

8. * ÷ 7 = 9

9. * x 7 = 42

10. 48 ÷ * = 8

11. 5 x * = 30

12. * ÷ 7 = 8

13. * x 9 = 27

14. 36 ÷ * = 9

15. 7 x * = 56

16. * ÷ 3 = 8

17. * x 9 = 72

18. 40 ÷ * = 8

19. 9 x * = 54

20. * ÷ 6 = 8

Super Tests

Congratulations!

If you are starting these **Super Tests** you must have done tests 1a to 15c in under 30 seconds. This is great stuff. You are now well on your way to becoming a **30 Second Champion**. You do these **Super Tests** in exactly the same way as the other tests, but this time you start with a time limit of 1 minute.

When you can do **Super Tests** 1a to 4c in under 1 minute, you start again. This time the time limit is 30 seconds.

When you have completed all the **Super Tests** in 30 seconds or less you will have become a **30 Second Champion**. *Brilliant!*

Complete the **30 Second Challenge Multiplying and Dividing Certificate** at the back of this book and show it to friends, teachers, parents and other relatives to admire.

The **Super Tests** may **look** really difficult when you first see them, but they are just as easy as the previous tests. Look at these examples:

1) 5×50

You know that $5 \times 5 = 25$.
So 5×50 is just 5 lots of 5 tens which is **25 tens or 250**. So 5×50 or $50 \times 5 = 250$.

2) $420 \div 6$

This is just as easy. You know that $42 \div 6 = 7$.
If there are 7 lots of 6 in 42, then there will be **70 lots of 6 in 420**. So $420 \div 6 = 70$.

3) $360 \div 40$

This is asking how many 4 tens are in 36 tens. In other words, how many 4s in 36? There are 9. So $360 \div 40 = 9$.

You are now ready to start
the Super Tests.

Best of luck!

Super Test 1a

1. $3 \times 20 = *$
2. $40 \times 7 = *$
3. $4 \times 30 = *$
4. $20 \times 8 = *$
5. $5 \times 40 = *$
6. $50 \times 2 = *$
7. $6 \times 50 = *$
8. $100 \times 4 = *$
9. $2 \times 80 = *$
10. $30 \times 4 = *$
11. $7 \times 30 = *$
12. $70 \times 6 = *$
13. $5 \times 50 = *$
14. $90 \times 4 = *$
15. $8 \times 60 = *$
16. $100 \times 10 = *$
17. $9 \times 20 = *$
18. $80 \times 5 = *$
19. $3 \times 90 = *$
20. $60 \times 6 = *$

Do not write in this space.

Place a sheet of scrap paper here and write your answers on that.

Always remember to time yourself for each test.

Write your score out of 20 and your time in minutes and seconds on the Record Sheet at the back of this book.

Super Test 1b

1. $160 \div 20 = *$

2. $250 \div 5 = *$

3. $100 \div 20 = *$

4. $120 \div 4 = *$

5. $360 \div 40 = *$

6. $300 \div 6 = *$

7. $400 \div 80 = *$

8. $200 \div 5 = *$

9. $280 \div 70 = *$

10. $180 \div 9 = *$

11. $360 \div 60 = *$

12. $270 \div 3 = *$

13. $400 \div 40 = *$

14. $210 \div 7 = *$

15. $420 \div 60 = *$

16. $160 \div 2 = *$

17. $1000 \div 100 = *$

18. $60 \div 3 = *$

19. $480 \div 60 = *$

20. $120 \div 30 = *$

Do not write in
this space.

Place a sheet of
scrap paper here
and write your
answers on that.

Always remember
to time yourself
for each test.

Write your score
out of 20 and
your time in
minutes and
seconds on the
Record Sheet
at the back of
this book.

Super Test 1c

1 $* \times 60 = 480$

2 $270 \div * = 3$

3 $80 \times * = 400$

4 $* \div 30 = 7$

5 $* \times 5 = 200$

6 $360 \div * = 90$

7 $8 \times * = 160$

8 $* \div 5 = 50$

9 $* \times 100 = 1000$

10 $120 \div * = 4$

11 $50 \times * = 300$

12 $* \div 40 = 7$

13 $* \times 6 = 360$

14 $180 \div * = 30$

15 $3 \times * = 120$

16 $* \div 70 = 6$

17 $* \times 4 = 400$

18 $60 \div * = 3$

19 $2 \times * = 160$

20 $* \div 2 = 50$

Do not write in this space.

Place a sheet of scrap paper here and write your answers on that.

Always remember to time yourself for each test.

Write your score out of 20 and your time in minutes and seconds on the Record Sheet at the back of this book.

Super Test 2a

1   $50 \times 6 = *$

2   $3 \times 70 = *$

3   $80 \times 3 = *$

4   $6 \times 80 = *$

5   $90 \times 5 = *$

6   $10 \times 70 = *$

7   $60 \times 2 = *$

8   $4 \times 90 = *$

9   $50 \times 7 = *$

10 $8 \times 80 = *$

11 $90 \times 9 = *$

12 $4 \times 20 = *$

13 $60 \times 4 = *$

14 $7 \times 90 = *$

15 $30 \times 8 = *$

16 $6 \times 90 = *$

17 $80 \times 7 = *$

18 $4 \times 60 = *$

19 $70 \times 5 = *$

20 $9 \times 60 = *$

Do not write in this space.

Place a sheet of scrap paper here and write your answers on that.

Always remember to time yourself for each test.

Write your score out of 20 and your time in minutes and seconds on the Record Sheet at the back of this book.

Super Test 2b

1   $450 \div 5 =$ *

2   $640 \div 80 =$ *

3   $240 \div 4 =$ *

4   $560 \div 7 =$ *

5   $630 \div 90 =$ *

6   $120 \div 2 =$ *

7   $480 \div 80 =$ *

8   $300 \div 6 =$ *

9   $540 \div 60 =$ *

10 $810 \div 9 =$ *

11 $700 \div 70 =$ *

12 $240 \div 3 =$ *

13 $80 \div 20 =$ *

14 $350 \div 5 =$ *

15 $360 \div 90 =$ *

16 $240 \div 8 =$ *

17 $240 \div 60 =$ *

18 $350 \div 7 =$ *

19 $210 \div 70 =$ *

20 $540 \div 90 =$ *

Super Test 2c

1   * x 90 = 360

2   240 ÷ * = 4

3   6 x * = 540

4   * ÷ 6 = 50

5   * x 5 = 450

6   810 ÷ * = 9

7   30 x * = 240

8   * ÷ 80 = 8

9   * x 3 = 210

10   240 ÷ * = 6

11   4 x * = 80

12   * ÷ 90 = 7

13   * x 80 = 560

14   700 ÷ * = 10

15   50 x * = 350

16   * ÷ 6 = 80

17   * x 5 = 350

18   540 ÷ * = 9

19   2 x * = 120

20   * ÷ 3 = 80

Do not write in this space.

Place a sheet of scrap paper here and write your answers on that.

Always remember to time yourself for each test.

Write your score out of 20 and your time in minutes and seconds on the Record Sheet at the back of this book.

Super Test 3a

1   $60 \times 100 = *$

2   $5 \times 30 = *$

3   $90 \times 7 = *$

4   $5 \times 80 = *$

5   $80 \times 4 = *$

6   $6 \times 30 = *$

7   $90 \times 3 = *$

8   $7 \times 70 = *$

9   $40 \times 5 = *$

10   $80 \times 9 = *$

11   $7 \times 40 = *$

12   $50 \times 9 = *$

13   $6 \times 70 = *$

14   $90 \times 8 = *$

15   $7 \times 20 = *$

16   $30 \times 6 = *$

17   $2 \times 90 = *$

18   $70 \times 8 = *$

19   $4 \times 80 = *$

20   $40 \times 4 = *$

Do not write in this space.

Place a sheet of scrap paper here and write your answers on that.

Always remember to time yourself for each test.

Write your score out of 20 and your time in minutes and seconds on the Record Sheet at the back of this book.

Super Test 3b

1 $490 \div 70 = *$

2 $180 \div 2 = *$

3 $280 \div 40 = *$

4 $320 \div 4 = *$

5 $630 \div 90 = *$

6 $720 \div 8 = *$

7 $180 \div 30 = *$

8 $6000 \div 60 = *$

9 $160 \div 4 = *$

10 $420 \div 70 = *$

11 $180 \div 6 = *$

12 $400 \div 80 = *$

13 $200 \div 5 = *$

14 $140 \div 20 = *$

15 $560 \div 8 = *$

16 $150 \div 30 = *$

17 $450 \div 9 = *$

18 $320 \div 80 = *$

19 $270 \div 3 = *$

20 $720 \div 9 = *$

Do not write in
this space.

Place a sheet of
scrap paper here
and write your
answers on that.

Always remember
to time yourself
for each test.

Write your score
out of 20 and
your time in
minutes and
seconds on the
Record Sheet
at the back of
this book.

Super Test 3c

1. $* \times 80 = 400$

2. $720 \div * = 9$

3. $7 \times * = 140$

4. $* \div 70 = 8$

5. $* \times 4 = 160$

6. $490 \div * = 7$

7. $6 \times * = 420$

8. $* \div 90 = 8$

9. $* \times 30 = 180$

10. $150 \div * = 5$

11. $60 \times * = 6000$

12. $* \div 4 = 80$

13. $* \times 6 = 180$

14. $630 \div * = 7$

15. $50 \times * = 450$

16. $* \div 40 = 7$

17. $* \times 5 = 200$

18. $270 \div * = 3$

19. $80 \times * = 320$

20. $* \div 2 = 90$

Do not write in this space.

Place a sheet of scrap paper here and write your answers on that.

Always remember to time yourself for each test.

Write your score out of 20 and your time in minutes and seconds on the Record Sheet at the back of this book.

Super Test 4a

1. $50 \times 30 = *$

2. $30 \times 70 = *$

3. $40 \times 80 = *$

4. $90 \times 50 = *$

5. $100 \times 100 = *$

6. $60 \times 80 = *$

7. $40 \times 40 = *$

8. $90 \times 70 = *$

9. $50 \times 80 = *$

10. $40 \times 60 = *$

11. $90 \times 90 = *$

12. $60 \times 70 = *$

13. $40 \times 90 = *$

14. $80 \times 70 = *$

15. $60 \times 50 = *$

16. $90 \times 30 = *$

17. $70 \times 50 = *$

18. $30 \times 60 = *$

19. $80 \times 80 = *$

20. $90 \times 60 = *$

Do not write in this space.

Place a sheet of scrap paper here and write your answers on that.

Always remember to time yourself for each test.

Write your score out of 20 and your time in minutes and seconds on the Record Sheet at the back of this book.

Super Test 4b

1   $2400 \div 60 = *$

2   $5600 \div 70 = *$

3   $1800 \div 60 = *$

4   $4800 \div 80 = *$

5   $5400 \div 60 = *$

6   $8100 \div 90 = *$

7   $1500 \div 30 = *$

8   $3600 \div 90 = *$

9   $6400 \div 80 = *$

10   $2100 \div 70 = *$

11   $4500 \div 50 = *$

12   $3000 \div 50 = *$

13   $4000 \div 80 = *$

14   $3500 \div 50 = *$

15   $6300 \div 70 = *$

16   $10,000 \div 100 = *$

17   $3200 \div 80 = *$

18   $2700 \div 30 = *$

19   $1600 \div 40 = *$

20   $4200 \div 70 = *$

Do not write in this space.

Place a sheet of scrap paper here and write your answers on that.

Always remember to time yourself for each test.

Write your score out of 20 and your time in minutes and seconds on the Record Sheet at the back of this book.

Super Test 4c

1 $* \times 50 = 4500$

2 $4000 \div * = 80$

3 $40 \times * = 1600$

4 $* \div 90 = 90$

5 $* \times 90 = 3600$

6 $2100 \div * = 70$

7 $90 \times * = 2700$

8 $* \div 80 = 80$

9 $* \times 60 = 5400$

10 $10,000 \div * = 100$

11 $40 \times * = 3200$

12 $* \div 60 = 70$

13 $* \times 50 = 3000$

14 $4800 \div * = 80$

15 $70 \times * = 3500$

16 $* \div 30 = 60$

17 $* \times 70 = 5600$

18 $1500 \div * = 50$

19 $40 \times * = 2400$

20 $* \div 70 = 90$

Do not write in this space.

Place a sheet of scrap paper here and write your answers on that.

Always remember to time yourself for each test.

Write your score out of 20 and your time in minutes and seconds on the Record Sheet at the back of this book.

Record Sheet

Date	Test No.	Time	Score

Record Sheet

Date	Test No.	Time	Score

Record Sheet

Date	Test No.	Time	Score

Record Sheet

Date	Test No.	Time	Score

Record Sheet

Date	Test No.	Time	Score